Expressions

Ranjitha Raj

BookLeaf Publishing

India | USA | UK

Presentation by *BookLeaf Publishing*

Web: www.bookleafpub.com

E-mail: info@bookleafpub.com

ISBN: 9789363312784

First edition 2024

This book is dedicated to all those who find solace and inspiration in the written word.

To my family, whose love sustains me through every chapter of life's journey.

To my friends, for their unwavering support and belief in my creative pursuits.

To the readers, who breathe life into these pages with their curiosity and empathy.

May these expressions resonate with your own stories and emotions, reflecting the enduring spirit within each of us.

ACKNOWLEDGEMENT

I'm deeply grateful to everyone who has joined me on this poetic journey.

To my family, friends, and readers, your open hearts give meaning to my expressions, enabling this journey of introspection and emotion.

I'm thankful for my life experiences, profession, and love for reading, which deepen my understanding of human emotions and shape my writing.

Heartfelt thanks to the dedicated team at BookLeaf Publishing for bringing *Expressions* to life.

I also thank all the driving forces, directly or indirectly, that have nurtured the poet within me.

PREFACE

In this collection of poems titled *Expressions*, I invite you to embark on this journey through the landscapes of emotion and introspection. Each poem is a reflection of moments cherished and lessons learned—moments that have shaped my understanding of life and the world around us.

Through these verses, I strive to capture the essence of human experience: from the gentle whispers of nature to the turbulent waves of emotion that define our existence. These poems are not just reflections of my personal journey but also an exploration of the shared human condition, where joy, sorrow, love, and solitude intertwine. I've used the first person in most of the poems to help readers connect these emotions to their own lives.

I believe that poetry has a unique ability to bridge the gap between the self and the world, offering solace in times of uncertainty and illumination in moments of clarity. My hope is that these poems resonate with you, offering a glimpse into the beauty of vulnerability and the power of resilience.

As you turn the pages of *Expressions*, may you find moments of connection, inspiration, and reflection. Thank you for joining me on this poetic journey.

With gratitude,

Ranjitha Raj

Table of contents

LOVE 13

UNCERTAINTY 20

PAIN 26

THE DARK 35

NATURE 43

REFLECTIONS 52

AWARENESS 63

THE LIGHT 76

LOVE

Imperfectly Perfect Love

It was a lovely morning, the world came alive
and seemed just right,
Everything was imperfectly perfect, bathed in
soft light.
My heart was singing, my soul danced so free,
My mind stood still, lost in daydream glee.

It was a heart day, a musical day.
As I was stepping out, I asked the mirror,
"Is everything okay?"
It smiled and kissed me gently, like my love
would convey.

Amongst the crowd, I searched for your gaze.
My heart raced, lost in a passionate haze.
I asked my phone screen,
"Is everything okay?"
It smiled and hugged me gently, like my love
would convey.

Your smile spoke volumes, your eyes told a tale,
An imperfectly perfect moment, beyond the veil.
So many firsts, a ride filled with silent noise,
Expressions of love in our unspoken voice.

There was so much to say, so much to share.
Every second cherished, I felt fresh and alive.
I asked my beating heart, bursting with
affection,
"Is everything okay?"
It danced with non-rhythmic perfection, just the
way you make me feel every day.

Throughout the day, I basked in love's tender
glow,
Holding it close, a treasure only my heart would
know.
A sense of belonging filled my being, a
comforting embrace.
So, I turned to my heart and asked with gentle
grace,
"Is everything okay?"
And my heart responded, its smile dancing with
desire,
Just as it does each day, filling me with joy and
delight,
Imperfectly perfect, in love's light.

The day drew to a close, a peaceful happiness in
my heart.
Returning home, I asked the mirror,
"Am I alright?"
With a loving kiss, it reassured my soul.
My heart sang and danced, feeling truly whole,

Just the way you make me feel every day.

Sitting on the balcony, reliving the moments,
Looking at the sky, and the magical fireflies,
Felt like nature dancing to my heart's tune.
Imperfectly perfect, these moments I hold,
Love's warmth and belonging, worth more than
gold.

"Is this forever?" the question that lingers,
Conflicts and doubts, where the heart often
lingers.
But my heart whispers, through joys and tears,
"It's better to have loved and lost," it declares.
For even in pain,
The joy of love is worth it, forever true,
Imperfectly perfect, this journey we walk,
With a heart that's touched, no regrets it holds.

As I lay on my bed, I ask myself,
"Is everything okay?"
His voice responds, love and hope,
With tender kisses and words that cope.
Assurance echoes, "Everything's okay,"
Bringing solace, and comfort my way.

My heart sings, dances, feeling complete,
With hope for a new day's sweet retreat.
Imperfectly perfect, it shall unfold,

Another day of wonders, yet untold.
Dreaming of a new day, with hope to behold,
Imperfectly perfect, its beauty will sway,
Embracing each moment, come what may.

You are the One

5

Heading to bed with a big smile,
I feel truly safe,
As if all my prayers have been answered,
And goodness fills my life.

It's the little things you do that make me feel so
special,
Bringing comfort and solace,
With no fear, just complete security.

Thankful to you and the universe,
I feel truly blessed.
You make me love myself even more,
What else could I wish for?

The happiness I feel in giving to you is hard to
describe,
Yet it's real and special, just for you.
In this joyful and serene moment,
I discover who I truly am.

Oasis of Love

My heart dances with butterflies,
In anticipation of meeting your eyes,
A journey of longing, feeling your caress,
Yearning to hold you, nothing less
My love, all I need is your love and warmth.

In your smile, I find a tender embrace,
Your gaze moves my soul, to a special place,
Your touch so new, never sensed or experienced
My love, all I need is your love and warmth.

I feel so secure and safe in your arms
A sense of belonging, a love that charms,
You have made me accept and love who I am,
To be myself, just true and raw
My love, all I need is your love and warmth.

When you call me beautiful, I blush,
World's color brightens,
A feeling of happiness and excitement
As if the world becomes more vibrant and
livelier
Lucky and blessed, that's how I feel,
You are the oasis in my life, so very real
My love, all I need is your love and warmth.

When you say you love me, I treasure it,
Because I know you mean it,
I see your depth through your eyes,
Though your words don't say much,
You speak through your eyes and expressions of
love,
I know I am cherished and important to you,
My love, all I need is your love and warmth.

Your touch, your kiss, igniting fire,
Yearning for more, the passion won't tire,
You are my constant thought, my everything,
Can't be without you, you are my heart's true
wing.
My love, all I need is your love and warmth.

I want you to know, you mean the world to me,
Breathing life, enjoying the ride,
With your love, I feel alive,
Savoring each moment by your side.

You make me love myself more,
Your love is not conditional,
It has no barriers and no boundaries,
Your love brings freedom, as I'd dreamed,
Which sets me free and everything I hoped for,
You made my fantasy turn into reality
My love, all I need is your love and warmth.

Cherished Treasures

You make me feel special every single day,
Like a fresh surprise each time you come my
way.
Every morning, I awaken to your love,
Uniquely expressed, as different as you are.

When our gazes meet, it's an intimate dance,
Your touch, a thrill only WE understand.
I feel blessed beyond measure to have this,
Our moments together beneath the moon's gentle
kiss.

With you, I feel like I'm on cloud nine,
A gift unmatched by any other, so fine.
Your presence, is a treasure, truly rare,
Especially the gift of your time, and care.

I cherish our cuddles, our playful times,
The sweetness of kisses, our passion's chimes,
And the unique bond that only we share,
In your arms, I find solace, and in your tight
hugs, warmth,
and how could I miss our endless talks on
everything under the sun?

I wouldn't trade these moments for anything,
They're the treasures I cherish endlessly.
You've painted my world with vibrant colors,
And so many firsts that are truly special,
Creating a tapestry of beauty unsurpassed.

We're fortunate to share this journey together,
Connected by a bond that feels like forever.
You have enriched my life with meaning, dear
For you are the one my heart has been longing
for.

Unspoken Words

Why is it, though you don't show what's inside,
I still feel my heart telling me you're on my
side?
Is it your own limits that keep you apart,
Or trouble with emotions that's hard on your
heart?

Maybe it's fear that makes you stay quiet,
Or something inside that you can't quite fight.
But deep down, I sense what you feel,
Even if you're unsure, it still seems real.

Your eyes and your face speak more than words,
Even when you don't say it, I've still heard.
It's okay, I get where you're coming from,
I understand, and I'm not here to run.

You're my precious gem, so dear and true,
And losing you is something I'd never do.
I won't misunderstand, or let you go,
You mean too much, more than you know.

Yearning for Healing

It's hard to see you in pain,
Life feels dull, nothing's the same.
Every day feels wrong, out of place,
All I want is to see your safe face.

Food doesn't taste good, no appetite,
Life's lost its color, its light.
Thoughts are confusing, clarity gone,
I'm tired, worried, from dusk till dawn.

Sleep evades, my heart weighs down,
I just want your healing to crown.
I pray and hope God will heed,
Our plea for help, our deepest need.

A swift recovery, my earnest plea,
May the world gleam brighter, for you and me.
Charm, color, and flavor, restored in light,
May everything shine, with renewed delight.

You!!

In every joy, you've stood by me,
In every tear, you've helped me see.
Your presence turns my days so bright,
With you, my world feels just right.

Vulnerably Yours

Is there anything that you don't know about me?
From every success to each sorrow's flow,
And all the little things in between,
Silly tales and stories we've seen.

In the tapestry of life, we've shared the threads,
With every joy I've told, our bond has spread.
Your presence, a light in both sun and shade,
In every triumph and sorrow, you've stayed.

Through the chapters of success, you've been my
cheer,
In moments of sorrow, you've held me near.
Each story shared, each joy retold,
Doubled in warmth, as our friendship unfolds.

Counting blessings, I find you there,
In every heartbeat, in every prayer.
Grateful for the moments, both big and small,
For in you, I've found a friend through it all.

My Companion

You are the reason I write,
You bring my words to life,
You spark the writer in me,
Through joy or strife.

Good days or bad,
Love or a fight,
Everything comes alive
When I set pen to paper at night.

At the end of the day,
I find a friend so true,
In the pages I create,
I never feel alone with you.

Beside You

Maybe I don't grasp your heart's full tune,
But I'm here to stand by you,
When you're troubled or feeling alone,
My care remains steadfast and true.

It pains me to see you distressed,
Though I may not fully understand,
Let me stay close, in your darkest hours,
Offering a comforting hand.

Even if my hold isn't perfect,
And my words sometimes miss the mark,
I'm here to share in your journey,
To walk with you through the dark.

Understanding Love

Everything made sense at last when you said,
"I'm not here to go away but to get along."
"I'm not leaving, just trying to connect."
I saw your love in those words,
"I'll make a small effort to meet you halfway,
While you ease your efforts and come closer to
where we meet."

What I understood was your love,
And how much I mean to you.
When you said you're here to get along,
Not to walk away, but to stay.

Love Never Dies

Every tragedy has sparked the writer in me,
Every heartbreak has awakened the poet within.
Each wounded soul
Has a story to tell.

I hope these words, someday,
Will heal and give hope to someone's heart.
Love never dies,
For I've etched it on paper forever.

Echoes of My Drama

It's curious how,
When I'm upset with you,
I turn to songs that speak of you,
And write words that revolve around you.

In these expressions,
I find a strange delight,
Feeling comfort as if your presence
Is woven through the melodies I write.

I end up talking to you,
As if all is fine,
In this peculiar comfort,
I find a happiness that's purely thine.

It's you, in these varied forms,
Helping me heal and cope,
Your essence guiding me softly,
Through every note and every hope.

Eternal Love

19

I don't believe in fairy tales,
For love is more than the dreams we chase.
It's the spark that stirs the heart,
A flame that keeps us from falling apart.

Love brings every emotion alive,
It's the reason we breathe, the will to survive.
It's the hope that keeps us going strong,
The silent wish we've carried all along.

Love, it never fades away,
In our hearts, it's here to stay.
Through all the storms, love will survive,
For love will always be alive.

UNCERTAINTY

In the Midst of Uncertainty

You are neither leaving me nor living with me,
Caught in the midst of uncertainty.
A presence felt, yet never fully near,
In the space between hope and fear.

Neither here nor gone, a lingering trace,
A silent presence, in this transient place.
Between the realms of heart and mind,
In this liminal space, where we both reside.

Who am I?

I believed I was special,
That I belonged,
That I was loved,
That I was cared for.
Then I realized it was all just a thought,
And thoughts need not be real.
They aren't facts,
Just illusions of my mind.
I wish my thoughts were real,
that I truly belonged to that special person
Who means everything to me.

As tears rolled down my cheeks,
Lying in bed, I pondered:
If my thoughts are my perception,
And if I don't belong,
Then who am I?

Head vs Heart

25

We strive for our heart, mind, and soul to align,
But it's a strange truth we struggle to define.
The heart seeks love, tender and true,
The mind chases success, in all that we do.
The soul yearns for peace, gentle and still,
Which one to choose, which desire to fulfill?
A profound dilemma we face every day,
Which part of ourselves will lead the way?

Cross Roads

I stand lost at a crossroads, unsure of which path
to choose.
Amidst the chaos in my mind, I opt for a journey
towards silence.
Venturing to a distant land, far from everyone
and everything familiar,
I contemplate disappearing for a while to
rediscover myself.

Stepping away from my routine,
breaking patterns and comfort zones,
I embrace encounters with strangers and
moments of reflection. Who am I?
Can I truly discover myself? Maybe.

Yet, with new exposures and experiences,
I know I will not return as the same person.
Finally, I glimpse a glimmer of hope at this
crossroad,
a promise of light guiding my way forward.

Tell me you don't mean it

27

No matter how honest you are,
Even when you say it's time to move on,
Why do I still hear a longing
In your voice, despite the harshest tones?

In every word that tells me to let go,
Why does a silent plea still show?
Why do your words seem to whisper,
"Stay with me, don't go"?

PAIN

Broken Promises

You promised wonders, bold and bright,
But led me blind, without a light.
Year after year, just pain to find,
Your limits kept me trapped in my mind.

If you choose not to chase your fate,
Why crush the dreams I strive to create?
Criticize, torment, and tear me down,
Each broken promise wore a frown.

But now as I rise, I'll break this chain,
Beyond your limits, past the pain.
I'll stand, I'll fight, I'll reach new heights,
And thrive beneath the endless lights.

Precious Pain

32

He asks me why I love so deeply, knowing it
brings pain,
But love is all I know, it's my heart's refrain.
It's the language I speak, the beat of my soul,
Even if it hurts, it's a price I'll gladly pay whole.

Loving and giving are all I understand,
For in heartache, there's truth that I can
withstand.
A fleeting touch makes every sorrow
worthwhile,
To be loved, even briefly, brings a warmth that
stays a while.
Love, in its purest form, is always worth the
while.

Expectations?

You expect so much from me,
To understand your feelings and words,
To see your situation, your intent,
And what your expressions mean.

But when I ask for something in return,
You say my needs are too high,
That they keep growing with time.

Yet didn't your own expectations rise,
To be understood in every way, just like mine?
In this dance of give and take,
Isn't it fair to seek the same?

Behind the Mask

Every word I speak now seems like a complaint,
an expectation, or a plea,
So, I wear a mask, hiding my true self behind a
smile.
You see me and think I am okay,
Yet your words cut through, unknowingly
breaking me.

In silence, I endure,
Suffering behind the facade I have created,
Where my pain remains hidden,
And the mask shields me from your sight.

I Wish

Despite you saying
You don't love me anymore,
I find it hard to accept,
My heart remains sore.

In my mind, it's always you,
And my heart can't let go,
I close my eyes and hope
That in dreams, you'll show.

I wish in my dreams
You could still be mine,
Where love isn't lost,
And everything is fine.
In that peaceful space,
I find the strength to heal.

Scars

If everything was fake,
Why did you break me so deep?
The fragments of my heart, shattered,
Too jagged to ever make a whole.

I gather them, trembling,
But each attempt only cuts deeper,
Bleeding, yet unable to heal,
I search for a Band-Aid to ease the pain.

But I've learned the truth, harsh and clear,
Band-Aids don't last, they only cover,
These scars, born from the broken pieces,
Will stay with me forever, a silent reminder.

Indifference

You say we're not soulmates,
Not meant to be together,
So, was our love just a fleeting spark,
A moment that didn't matter?

I'm angry, I'm hurt—
How can you be so cold?
Was it all just a lie,
This bond we thought so bold?

Did it mean nothing at all,
Those whispers in the dark?
Now I'm left with only questions,
And a heart that bears the mark.

The Bad Side of a Good Thing

It makes me wonder
If my mental health struggles
Are a hidden blessing.
When I'm at my worst,
The writer within me comes alive.

I write,
And it's writing that soothes me,
Relieves my pain,
And lets me vent.
Catharsis happens,
And I feel at ease.

But then I wonder,
Do I write because I have no one to talk to?
Isn't it also a reality that I'm lonely?
Moments of joy turn back to pain,
In an endless loop.

So should I be glad that writing helps me and sparks my creativity,
Or should I grieve the fact that I have no one to talk to?

THE DARK

Castle on My Grave

You built a castle upon my grave,
Happy with her, your heart's newfound rave.
Gazing into her eyes with no remorse,
For I let you go, love's painful course.

No guilt or regret weighs upon you,
For I never made you feel small.
I know the pain of being unloved,
Abandoned without fault.

No remorse met my broken heart,
Conveniently shattered by your part.
You never sought to ease my pain,
And left me alone in the pouring rain.

Busy building your castle high,
Unaware, on my grave you rely.
I closed my eyes, tears flowed free,
Supporting you, burying me.

Beneath the weight of your steps, I lay,
Voice unheard, fading away.

Void

Amid my darkness and depression,
Some days I'm happy, some days I'm lost,
My loved ones see a smile and think I'm fine,
But inside, I'm sensitive, teetering on the edge,
Ready to break, though they believe I can bear it
all.

All I crave is to belong, to be understood,
Yet all I hear is that I'm mature enough
To process, to handle, to withstand it all.
But I lack the strength to argue, to fight,
To make you see how much I need you here.

I've lost the trust to confide, to express,
If my words, my feelings, and actions can't
convince you,
What more can I say? I'm losing hope,
Day by day, torn between what is right and what
is wrong,
Unsure of what to share, how much to share,
How vulnerable I can afford to be.

I'm tired, I can't think anymore,
You don't seem to understand, not really.
I'm weary of explaining my darkness,

I just want to retreat, to my shell,
And let the universe take over, whatever that
means.

I don't know where to turn, whom to trust,
To whom can I share my joys and sorrows?
In a world where betrayal and broken promises
are common,
You lied when you said you'd be there,
To support me, to see my goals through.

Now, everything feels meaningless, shattered,
I've reached a point where explanations are
empty,
Where I no longer want to fight, argue, explain,
I don't want to be vulnerable anymore.
My heart aches, and you don't seem to
understand.

I want to go silent, away from everyone,
To be alone, wrapped in my own stillness.
It's the worst feeling, being shown the bright
sky,
Only to be plunged into darkness by the same
hand.
I no longer believe in silver linings,
I'm descending into the darkness, deeper and
deeper,
Where trust fades, and I see no one, feel no one.

Somewhere in the Middle of Depression

In shadows where it started, lost in time,
A creeping darkness, subtle and sublime.
I functioned through the days, dismissing the
signs,
Ignored the sleepless nights and dwindling lines.

A noise within my mind, a constant churn,
A fire of thoughts that ceaselessly burn.
I drift away from voices, hearts, and hands,
In silence, feeling no one understands.

The world is draped in shadows, all seems gray,
Loved ones too distant, in disarray.
A void within, an empty, darkened space,
Where hope is but a whisper, hard to trace.

Fading slowly, life's edges blur and blend,
The pain so deep, it beckons for an end.
Yet in the faces of the ones I love,
I find a fragile strength, a light above.

Guilt and helplessness weigh me down,
But living for them helps me carry on.
I fight my thoughts, my inner strife,
Searching for light and purpose in life.

How long this battle continues, I don't know,
But in this journey, strength and hope will grow.
Through darkness, I will strive to find my way,
Towards a dawn that brings a brighter day.

Broken

I think and think and think,
And deep down, I feel you're as broken as I am,
Yearning for love and touch.
I sense you're finding comfort and solace in me,
Looking for that missing piece.

Sometimes, my own pain consumes me,
Blinding me to yours.
My tears have made you hide behind a mask.
In the journey of you empowering me,
I see you sinking deeper into your own pain.

I want to help you, save you,
But my darkness overwhelms me,
And I end up hurting you.
My illness makes me negative,
And your helplessness to save me
Is drowning you.

Please know that deep down, I understand you.
I'm not pushing you away.
I've said mean things,
But I can't live without you.
You're someone I don't want to lose.

I hope we can weather this storm and stay together,
Until the end of our lives.
Not sure if it will be a happily ever after,
But definitely not without each other.
I need you.

NATURE

City Lights and New Insights

As I find myself standing on the 17th-floor
balcony,
an unusual experience for someone who has
always cherished the allure of independent
houses,
I am pleasantly surprised.

Today, I am enchanted by the captivating view
and the vibrant city lights, surpassing even the
brilliance of the stars and the moon.

The gentle breeze caresses my body as I
indulge in a cup of hot tea,
accompanied by the melodies of romantic songs.

These simple pleasures fill my heart with joy,
adorning my lips with a smile and transforming
this moment into something truly special and
perfect.
From this lofty vantage point,
I gain a new perspective akin to that of a bird
soaring above.

It prompts me to contemplate how often

we confine ourselves within our own beliefs and
limitations,
unknowingly accepting them as absolute truths.
We neglect the wondrous possibilities and
experiences
that lie on the other side,
failing to embrace the beauty they offer.

The Therapeutic Crunch

55

As I step onto the dried leaves scattered across
the forest floor,
I am immediately greeted by the soft crunching
sound of the leaves
beneath my feet.
The crispness of the leaves, brittle from the lack
of moisture,
creates a satisfying sensation with each step I
take.

The rustling of the leaves beneath my feet fills
the air,
and I feel as though I am part of the natural
world around me.
The leaves are of varying sizes and shapes,
some brown and curled up, others still green and
partially intact.
As I walk, I cannot help but marvel at the
intricate patterns and textures that nature has
created.

The earthy aroma of the leaves mingles with the
scent of fresh air,
and I take deep breaths in, savoring the clean
and pure fragrance.

The sound of birds chirping and leaves rustling
in the gentle breeze is soothing,
and I feel a sense of calm and tranquility wash
over me.

As I continue my walk, I find myself lost in
thought,
pondering the beauty of the natural world
and how fortunate I am to be able to experience
it.
The dried leaves beneath my feet are a reminder
of the cycle of life and the changing seasons,
and I am grateful for this moment of connection
with nature.

Whispers of Happiness

As I opened the door and saw the moon, a smile
lit up my face.
It brought back the same joy I felt as a child
while gazing at the sky.
My inner child soaked in everything, the fresh
scent of jasmine,
the beauty of the stars and the vast moonlit sky.

Today, everything feels so happy,
with love all around and the hope of new
beginnings.
It's a beautiful world, and I'm just so happy to be
alive,
enjoying the refreshing hug of nature.

I sense a strong connection,
a feeling of belonging.
Words can't quite capture how deeply I'm
connected to nature;
it's beyond any measure.
Sharing this joy with my beloved feels like a
true blessing.

Concrete Jungle

She finds the wild forests, where things are
imperfect but REAL, fascinating,
whereas most people are enchanted with the
Perfect, Beautiful Garden in the Concrete
Jungle.

She believes that because life is not a
straight line; instead it's filled with ups and
downs,
Just like nature's unpredictable rhythm,
perfection is merely an ILLUSION.

Nature's Mirror

Nature stands as a mirror clear,
With scars and beauty intertwined,
It gives with open arms,
And endures, gentle and kind.

It moves at its own steady pace,
No rush, no race to claim,
With no expectations,
Yet it teaches us the same.

Nature's love is patient,
A harmony that's true,
We are all one in its embrace,
Connected through and through.

Yet humans often fight and quarrel,
Ignoring lessons in the breeze,
Why, when nature shows us peace,
Do we struggle to find ease?

In nature's calm and steady flow,
There's wisdom we could come to know.
If only we would learn its way,
And find our peace in each new day.

Nature - The Teacher

Nature teaches us every day,
No matter what, it finds a way.
We take, we hurt, but it still gives,
With a love that endlessly lives.

This is the secret of love's deep core,
No matter what, it always gives more.
Through ups and downs, it stays so strong,
In love, we find where we belong.

We do anything to bring back the light,
To see that smile, to make things right.
For love, like nature, always cares,
And in its warmth, everything repairs.

REFLECTIONS

Loneliness VS Solitude

Surrounded by silence, I feel all alone,
No one seems to care, my heart turns to stone.
No caring voices seem to come near,
My chest constricts with anxious fear.
My loved ones, it seems, don't try to convey,
And make no effort to show I'm not alone.

I'm filled with anger, frustration, sadness, and
tears,
Mixed feelings churn within, fueling my fears.
Am I too negative or expecting too much?
Am I on the wrong path, missing a proper
touch?
Have I ever made the right choices and decisions
as such?

I once found peace in quiet and solitude's grace,
But loneliness hits differently, puts me out of
place.
I feel lost in this world, like I don't belong,
A sense of hopelessness, helplessness so strong.
Does that mean I can't help myself, embrace my
own space?
Lots of questions, too much thinking, it's all a
mess.

Makes me feel lost and in distress,
I want to be strong, deep down I know I am,
I wish for someone's hand in moments of
despair.

In the darkest hours, I hope for a voice so kind,
To say, "It'll be alright, peace you will find."
Then I can trust in me, stand strong and tall,
Knowing that I'm loved, I won't fear the fall.

As I reflect, maybe the future holds a brighter
sight,
A world where things get better, where
everything feels right.
Just like the day following the night's embrace,
A beautiful world where love finds its place.

Do I need to do everything on my own? No, not
really.
Is it fine to ask for some help? Yes, absolutely.
I think this silence and loneliness will go away,
And there will be a day when I'll enjoy solitude
and being alone again.

Rat Race

Looking at the sky, birds return to their homes
and nests,
It makes me wonder why humans toil long hours
without rest.
With artificial lights, we extend our work into
the night,
But at what cost do we chase after money's
might?

Though working late may seem a sign of
dedication bold,
Are we not straying from nature's rhythm, so
ancient and old?
Pushing limits, indeed, but at the cost of our
health and peace,
Is this relentless pursuit not where our troubles
increase?

Let us question the path we take under artificial
light,
Does it steer us away from well-being, into
endless night?
For in the quiet of natural order, may lie the key,
To balance work and rest, to live in harmony and
free.

Solitude

In solitude's embrace, I discover myself,
Amidst the quiet, where thoughts find shelf.
No distractions to pull me astray,
Just the rhythm of my breath, guiding my way.

In the silence, my mind finds its calm,
Echoes of my thoughts, like a healing balm.
I listen closely to my heart's soft beat,
In this peaceful solitude, I feel complete.

Here, I unravel layers of who I am,
Embracing my flaws, like an open palm.
Solitude reveals my strengths and fears,
Guiding me towards clearer, calmer years.

In the stillness, I find my deepest truth,
A connection to myself, ageless and uncouth.
Solitude and silence, my trusted allies,
Where I discover myself, beneath life's guise.

FOMO

I wonder, in this fast-paced world,
Where competition is fierce,
And FOMO drives us all,
We strive to achieve everything,
Willing to do whatever it takes.

But at what cost?
If we lose ourselves along the way,
Is it really worth it?
We often forget who we're becoming,
As we chase after every goal.

Am I okay with giving up my values,
Sacrificing my health,
And trading away my peace of mind?
It's something worth considering.

Success gained this way isn't true success.
So I choose to step back,
Away from the noise and the crowd,
To define success in my own way—
Not by money,
But by what truly matters to me.

Face the Fear

Fear of ending up alone,
Of being abandoned,
Makes us wear false masks,
And endure what's unkind.

We put up with abuse,
Swallow what's toxic,
All to avoid the pain
Of being alone.

It makes me wonder:
But why are we so scared
To befriend ourselves,
To live with our thoughts
And make a fresh start?

In nature's gentle calm,
Being alone is not a strain,
Instead, we find solace,
And solitude heals the pain,
And makes us feel whole again.

Connection

I'm broken,
And I know you are too.
I express my pain,
While you keep it in.
Your feeling of helplessness
Makes me feel helpless too.

If you're not okay,
Nothing inside me feels right,
And our bond suffers too.
I need you as much as you need me.

But in all the chaos and fights,
We've forgotten to listen to our hearts.
In the quiet moments, when I ask what my heart wants,
It whispers 'US'—that's YOU and ME.

Lessons from Darkness

Nothing in life has taught me more
Than heartbreak, rejection, and failure's sting,
Disappointment, betrayal, and loss,
Loneliness, fear, anxiety, and everything they
bring.

These shadows, once feared and fought,
Now reveal their hidden gifts.
As I grew, I saw their strength,
Building resilience where pain once lived.

In facing these deep emotions,
I discovered strength and wisdom to thrive.
They sculpted me into who I am,
Teaching me the true lessons of life.

Now I greet failures with an open heart,
Welcoming them as part of my growth.
In every challenge, I uncover strength,
That leads me forward, guiding my path.

Let Go

We never seem to understand,
Sometimes it's not the person we cling to,
It's the feeling that keeps us holding on,
Even when the relationship has soured.

We try to recreate that feeling,
Which is no longer a reality.
Let go…

AWARENESS

Disillusioned

I was never a priority,
Never important, never needed,
An illusion I clung to, alone,
Lost in shadows I thought were light.

Now my eyes have opened wide,
Seeing clearly what I denied,
Slowly coming to terms with truth,
A bitter pill that stings the soul.
It hurts, a deep and quiet ache,
But this is my reality,
No longer blinded by false hopes,
I embrace the pain and set it free.

Why is that I am always wrong?

I gave my heart so freely,
Thought your love was true,
But I was wrong.
I loved you so much,
And I thought you loved me too,
But my heart sinks and aches when you say
It's *me* who is always wrong.

Why's my pain invisible to you?
Though I've shared it repeatedly
Why, did you never try, to understand the tears I
cry,
Despite sharing with you repeatedly, how lonely
I feel
And why is it ok for you to be this way?
And why is it that I'm always wrong?

You placed your habits and addictions first,
And you see no fault in yourself,
Ignored me every day,
But when I reached out to others,
Insecurity found its way,
I craved your love, your validation,
Yet I'm the one you led astray.
Why is that I'm always wrong?

I tried multiple ways to express and
communicate how I feel
I spoke my truth, so many times,
Yet you were deaf to my desperate cries,
What more can I do to make this work?
Why is it that I'm always wrong?

Did you never feel,
The love I had, so raw and real?
I waited for change, hope in my heart,
But you only pushed me further apart.
Why is that you neither live with me nor leave
me
If I'm all that bad and wrong?

Why is that you never felt like living or being
with me
I have been forever waiting with hope that
things will change
I changed myself too
But you broke me down, piece by piece,
You criticized me, you shattered me
And you said I'm no good
Why is that I'm always wrong?

I did everything to help you, support you
Take care of you, to understand you

But you questioned my commitment, my duties,
and responsibilities
When I know I never failed to do my duties
Can you tell me why is that I'm not good
I'm more desperate to know now
And I deserve to know it,
Why is that I'm always wrong?

Countless questions I have for you
To which you have no answers
And your claim of being right doesn't soothe my
ache,
Each time I try to talk to you
You twist it all, laying blame on my side,
How can mistakes solely in me reside?
Why is that I'm always painted as wrong?
In this endless cycle, where I don't belong?

A decade passed, I'm now so numb,
Nothing matters to me anymore
I no longer seek to conform to your idea of
goodness
I no more will be a slave to my values
I deserve to be happy
I deserve to live
I deserve to be loved
And I know I'm NOT WRONG.

Paradox of the Heart

In us lies a conflict, deep and strong,
A need to belong, yet crave solitude's song.
We desire to possess the world entire,
Yet yearn for the simplicity of nothing to aspire.

We ache to love with all our might,
Yet long to detach, to take flight.
A strange paradox, so vivid and bright,
Such are the complexities that life brings to
light.

Fear's Flight

I lived with the fear of failure's sting,
Abandonment, loss, and rejection's ring.
So I settled for less, staying low,
Letting fear dictate where I'd go.

But now the truth shines clear and bright—
It was fear that chased me, hidden from sight.
I've decided to take away its power,
Raising my bar, hour by hour.

Standing firm and strong, I rise,
As fear's grip begins to compromise.
With its leaving, life opens wide,
I welcome the new with hope as my guide.

Helpless

When you told me you were leaving,
I never thought about how much it hurt you.
In my own sorrow,
I didn't see that your heart could break too.

You tried to show your pain,
But I was too lost in my own tears to notice.
Now, as I reflect and feel,
I realize you too were helpless to help both you
and me.

Understanding Boundaries

I hated the boundaries you set,
They felt like walls that made you distant,
I thought you were now far away,
Lost beyond the reach of my sight.

But now I understand,
As I navigate the depths,
Boundaries are not barriers,
They are bridges to our own well-being.

They're not meant to shut others out,
But to safeguard our own selves.
Boundaries create space for us to breathe,
And keep us balanced and whole.

Inner Wisdom

Nothing came from outside,
All my answers were within.
The quieter and calmer I became,
The stronger my inner voice grew.

In the stillness of my mind,
It spoke with clarity and grace,
Guiding me through tough times,
And helping me find my way.

With each moment of calm,
My inner strength became clear,
Guiding me through life's challenges,
With a voice I learned to hear.

Awakening

81

I was a victim,
Blaming the world and you,
Caught in a cycle of despair,
Where my pain felt so true.

I sought to control,
To shape life to my will,
Yet in my striving and reaching,
I found only a void to fill.

Then it came to surrender,
A letting go of the fight,
Everything fell into place,
In the soft embrace of light.

Awakening dawned upon me,
A clarity so profound,
And in that newfound freedom,
Nothing else could be found.

Moving Ahead

People say, "Let go, forgive,"
I say, "I can't," for I've been hurt.
I've felt the pain and the sting,
But will dwelling on it change anything?

I've learned the truth I needed to know,
Acceptance helps me face the blow.
I must embrace what's happened as real,
And take action to heal and feel.

No longer a victim of what's past,
I choose to rise, to be strong at last.
I'm not defined by what was done to me,
But by the steps I take to be free.

THE LIGHT

The Art of Listening

When loved ones share their woes or pain,
It's not always for solutions to gain.
Their words may flow like a gentle stream,
Not for fixing, but for you to glean.

They're not seeking answers or a plan,
Just someone to listen, to understand.
So, pause your thoughts and hear their plea,
For in your silence, their hearts find ease.

Don't rush to mend or to correct,
Sometimes it's just their hearts that reflect.
So let them speak, and simply be there,
For in listening, you show that you care.

Values: Chains or Compass?

85

Values guide our choices, shape our path,
Yet they can ensnare us in their grasp.
When we become slaves to their command,
We lose freedom to reach, to understand.

Let values be a compass, not a chain,
To serve us well, and help us gain.
For when we serve with purpose true,
We find our dreams and goals to pursue.

The Power of Words

86

Be careful with your words, for they may linger,
Repeating in minds with a persistent finger.
Once spoken, they echo and replay,
In hearts and minds, night and day.

Words can linger, and subtly stay,
In someone's mind, throughout the day.
So choose your words with care and grace,
For they echo in others' inner space.

Present Tense

Why do we dwell on days gone by,
Or dream of futures yet to fly?
The present slips right through our hands,
We forget to cherish life's small strands.

We hold each moment, grasping tight,
But why not enjoy its fleeting light?
Regret fills us when it's no more,
We lose the joy we should adore.

Complaints and critiques fill our days,
Comparing lives in countless ways.
What we lack, we always see,
Ignoring what's here, our reality.

In chasing dreams or past's embrace,
Life rushes by, a rapid pace.
We've forgotten how to live,
To appreciate and simply give.

Let's embrace the now, in every breath,
Before it slips away in death.
Cherish moments, let them be,
In the present, live fully, free.

Living Now

We lose so much thinking about the past,
And worrying about the future that's vast.
Can we shift from *doing* to just *being*?
For nothing lasts forever, this truth is freeing.

Enjoy the present, where strength lies,
In the now, where happiness flies.

From Scars to Strength

In my scars and failures, I found my way,
Resilience blossomed with each setback's sway.
Every fall taught me to stand,
Leading me closer to where I planned.

Failures mold me, nothing to dread,
Each scar a mark where courage is bred.
With every stumble, I learn and grow,
Failures don't stop me—they help me know
The path to where I'm meant to go.

Acceptance

Why do we always wait in vain,
For those who caused our deepest pain?
Their words and actions cut so deep,
Yet still, for them, our hopes we keep.

Even shattered into pieces small,
We hope they'll see and hear our call.
We wait for them to say they're sorry,
Believing they'll ease our weary worry.

Why do we think they'll feel our ache,
And mend the hearts they chose to break?
It's not the ones who caused the scar,
Who'll heal our wounds and take us far.

Let go, embrace the love that's true,
From those who care and cherish you.
Open your heart to their warm embrace,
And find the healing in their grace.

Maturity

Don't judge past choices by today's demands,
For each decision was made with the best of
plans.
Yesterday's needs shaped the paths you took,
Each choice was a chapter in a well-worn book.

The past decisions met the needs of then,
Guided by the knowledge you had back then.
So, when you look back, don't cast blame or
shame,
For each decision was right in the time it came.

Today, face the present with clarity and grace,
Make choices that meet your current pace.
Don't compare to what once was done,
For the past was its own journey, and now it's
gone.

What you knew before was all you could see,
And those past decisions were right for thee,
So, make today's choices with fresh insight,
Respect the past, and set your future bright.

Unmet Needs

Your unhappiness hides in unmet needs,
The ache within comes from what it seeks.
The things you long for but cannot find,
Are what leave your heart feeling behind.

Listen to your quiet, restless sigh,
It's your needs reaching out, asking why.
To find your peace and ease your mind,
Understand what you need to leave behind.

Reach for purpose, chase what you desire,
Express your needs, ignite your inner fire.
Set clear goals, let your heart's truth lead,
And move forward with hope as your creed.

Oversharing

93

Be cautious where your secrets roam,
Sharing with those who may not be your own.
Too much revealed to those untrue,
Can turn your trust into a tool they'll use.

Unconcerned ears may twist and bend,
Your private thoughts they might offend.
Protect your heart and what you say,
Not all are kind in how they play.

Yet sharing with those who truly care,
Who hold your trust with love and flair,
Is not a risk but a bond so true,
With loved ones who wish the best for you.

Self-esteem

94

Don't let their voices drown your spark,
Or their eyes pull you into the dark.
Hold your worth close, like a guiding star,
Stay true to yourself, no matter how far.

In chasing their praise, don't lose your way,
Remember your value, come what may.
Let your light shine, bold and bright,
For in your own truth, you'll find your light.

Caged Love

In the name of love, you hold them near,
Sheltering them from every fear.
But in your hold, they start to fade,
Yearning for light in the shadow you've made.

Overprotecting, you think you care,
Yet their spirits wither in the stifling air.
You believe you guard them from the storm,
But they long to step out, to feel life's form.

True love is not a cage, but a breeze,
That lets them soar with graceful ease.
Teach them to carry their own umbrella,
To face the rain, and discover their strength.

For how long will you shield them from strife?
Let them embrace the trials of life.
True love means watching them grow,
As they find their path, in the world they know.

Let them bloom, let them be free,
For in their growth, your love will see.
That letting go is the greatest art,
Of loving fully, with an open heart.

Decisions

To change or stay the same,
There's always a cost, that's the game.
We might complain or point the blame,
But choices are ours, all the same.

Whether we stay and grumble along,
Or face the cost and move on strong,
The path is ours to take or leave,
And in our choices, we must believe.

Instead of blaming what's tough,
Embrace the choice, though it's rough.
The path we take is in our hands,
And in our choices, we make our stand.

Aftermath

In love and marriage, high hopes may sting,
When expectations soar too high,
Disappointment and hurt begin to cling,
As reality falls short of the sky.

When we seek too much from each passing day,
From partners we cherish and adore,
We set the stage for heartache's play,
And joy seems distant, less and more.

Yet when we adjust our hopes and dreams,
And accept love's ebb and flow,
We find a bond that gently redeems,
And our hearts start to warmly glow.

By easing expectations and embracing what's
real,
We find peace on our shared path,
Love grows deeper when we simply feel,
And treasure each moment's simple aftermath.

Judge the Judgements

Whenever they judge, blame, or express their
view,
Remember this truth as you see it through:
I'm not what they perceive,
Nor the image they choose to believe.

Their words about me are mere reflections,
Shaped by their own life's projections.
What they say is just a shadow,
Cast from their limited view,
A projection of their perception,
Not the essence of who I am, true.

In the mirror of their mind,
I'm shaped by their own lens,
But beyond their fleeting gaze,
There's a truth that never bends.

So, hold this close when you ponder what they
see,
I'm more than their reflections,
I'm who I am, and who I choose to be.

The Inner Guide

Within each, a force resides, wise and true,
A life force, universal, that we all pursue.
Deep within, it whispers with clarity,
An inner knowing, our intuitive key.

Through intuition, this wisdom unfolds,
Guiding us, as our story unfolds.
In every moment, it speaks its truth,
A source of knowledge from our youth.

Listen closely to this inner voice,
For it knows what's right, our inner choice.
Trust in its guidance, clear and bright,
The universal wisdom, our guiding light.

Attached, Yet Unattached

I seek to be attached, yet unattached,
To avoid disappointment and regret.
With fewer expectations,
And less trust in the world,
I find strength and abilities within.
No room for betrayal from the world,
In this newfound understanding, I love freely,
Savoring love's pure joy,
Embracing attachment, yet remaining
unattached.